W9-AAE-086

ALTERNATOR
BOOKS™

THE
WOMEN'S
RIGHTS
MOVEMENT

ERIC BRAUN

Lerner Publications ◆ Minneapolis

Lerner Publications Company
A division of Lerner Publishing Group, Inc.
241 First Avenue North
Minneapolis, MN 55401 USA

For reading levels and more information, look up this title at
www.lernerbooks.com.

Main body text set in Aptifer Slab LT Pro Regular 11.5/18.
Typeface provided by Linotype AG.

Library of Congress Cataloging-in-Publication Data

Names: Braun, Eric, 1971 author.
Title: The women's rights movement / Eric Braun.
Description: Minneapolis : Lerner Publications,
    [2018] | Series: Movements that matter (Alternator Books) | Includes
    bibliographical references and index.
Identifiers: LCCN 2017039395 (print) | LCCN 2017047371 (ebook) |
    ISBN 9781541525580 (eb pdf) | ISBN 9781541523326 (lb : alk. paper)
Subjects: LCSH: Feminism—United States—History—Juvenile
    literature. | Women's rights—United States—History—Juvenile
    literature.
Classification: LCC HQ1410 (ebook) | LCC HQ1410 .B725 2018 (print) |
    DDC 323.3/4—dc23

LC record available at https://lccn.loc.gov/2017039395

Manufactured in the United States of America
1-44405-34664-1/17/2018

CONTENTS

NO MORE MISS AMERICA!

Inside the Atlantic City, New Jersey, convention center, the Miss America beauty pageant is under way. Outside, a few hundred women gather to express their disapproval. These **activists** hold signs demanding that women not be judged solely for their bodies. They toss bras, high heels, and makeup into a trash can.

Activists speaking out against the Miss America pageant sit amid signs expressing their objections.

WELCOME TO THE MISS AMERICA CATTLE AUCTION

The 1960s was a time of heated activism, from marches supporting rights for women and African Americans to sit-ins objecting to war.

Several activists make their way inside. They unfurl a bedsheet with a message: "Women's Liberation." But they don't stay long. Police escort them out. News of the **protest** spreads, though. Soon people everywhere are talking about women's liberation.

This 1968 scene was a memorable part of the women's rights movement in the 1960s. The movement has a rich history of people fighting for fair treatment of women. Women's rights activists have fought for women's voting rights, workplace equality, **economic** independence, and more.

CHAPTER 1

WE WANT TO VOTE

The women's rights movement didn't begin with any single event. But in the United States, historians sometimes name 1848 as the beginning of what's often called the first wave of the movement. That summer two groundbreaking activists, Elizabeth Cady Stanton and Lucretia Mott, organized the world's first women's rights convention in Seneca Falls, New York. They wrote a document called the Declaration of Sentiments. In it, they declared thirteen rights that they wanted women to have—including the right to vote, which women didn't have at that time.

Elizabeth Cady Stanton was a strong voice for women's rights from the mid-nineteenth century to her death in 1902.

JOINING FORCES

In 1851 Stanton began working with Susan B. Anthony, an **abolitionist**. Both activists felt the rights of women and the rights of slaves were closely tied. But when the Fifteenth Amendment to the US Constitution granted African American men the right to vote in 1870, it didn't include women. Stanton and Anthony moved away from the abolitionist movement to focus only on women's rights.

Susan B. Anthony was raised in the Quaker faith, which traditionally supports equality between men and women.

Many early women's rights advocates, such as these women, sought to outlaw alcohol. They believed alcohol harmed women and children by hurting family finances and making some men more prone to violence.

To fight for the right to vote, or **suffrage**, they formed the National Woman Suffrage Association (NWSA) in 1869. At first, they had trouble building support. But by the 1880s, more people were behind the cause. Many supporters were part of the **temperance** movement, which sought to outlaw alcoholic beverages. With growing support, Stanton and Anthony merged their group with another suffrage group to form the National American Woman Suffrage Association (NAWSA) in 1890.

CHANGING LAWS

NAWSA worked to change state laws instead of federal laws about voting. They felt this was the only way to achieve success. But by 1910, only five states had passed laws giving women voting rights. Some suffragists were frustrated with this slow progress. In 1913 an up-and-coming suffragist named Alice Paul formed a group called the Congressional Union for Woman Suffrage. They were more radical than NAWSA. They held marches demanding the right to vote.

Alice Paul supported the same causes as earlier activists, but she wanted to see women's rights advance more quickly.

Woodrow Wilson served as US president from 1913 to 1921.

The combined efforts of both groups paid off. By January 1918, President Woodrow Wilson was a suffrage supporter and officially agreed to support women's voting rights.

Congress began working on an amendment granting women the right to vote. The Nineteenth Amendment became law in 1920—more than seventy years after those first activists gathered in Seneca Falls. The first wave of the women's rights movement had achieved a major goal.

Women proudly cast their ballots to make their voices heard.

CHAPTER 2

WE WANT EQUAL RIGHTS

Although women had the right to vote, they didn't have equality. Many were expected to do whatever their husbands or fathers told them to do. They were often offered only jobs that men didn't want. And they were usually paid less for their work. They couldn't make large purchases or open credit card or bank accounts without the permission of their husband or father.

These women work at factory jobs in 1943.

The women's rights movement was no longer focused mainly on one goal, as it had been with suffrage. It now had a broader goal, but the cause kept making progress. Between 1900 and 1930, the percentage of female college graduates in the United States doubled. During World War II (1939–1945), while men were away in the armed services, some women got paying jobs for the first time. And by the 1950s, women such as Rosa Parks were playing lead roles in the **civil rights movement** aimed at gaining equality for African Americans.

Rosa Parks, who worked as a seamstress to support herself, broke barriers as an activist who was both female and African American. She was a key voice in the fight for rights for black Americans.

SHAKING THINGS UP

By the 1960s, the civil rights movement had made protests a part of American life. This movement inspired a second wave of women's rights activists. And when the Civil Rights Act of 1964 passed, it included Title VII. This law prohibited **discrimination** in the workplace based on gender.

In fact, the 1960s was a decade of huge change for women. In 1963 writer and activist Betty Friedan published *The Feminine Mystique.* The book criticized society's view of women as wives and homemakers. That same year, the Equal Pay Act made it illegal for women to be paid less than men.

In addition to ending workplace gender discrimination, the Civil Rights Act of 1964 led to the racial integration of many schools. Here two girls in a recently integrated school size each other up.

In 1966 Friedan and twenty-seven others formed the National Organization for Women (NOW). NOW wanted to advance women's rights and to make sure the government enforced existing laws. NOW felt that the government wasn't doing enough to enforce the Civil Rights Act and the Equal Pay Act.

A Moment in the Movement

Passing and enforcing women's rights laws has been an uphill climb. For example, Alice Paul proposed the Equal Rights Amendment in 1923. It aimed to end discrimination based on gender in employment, banking, and other legal matters. To become law, the amendment needed congressional approval. Then it needed two-thirds of the states to approve it.

From the 1920s through the 1960s, nothing much happened with the amendment. Then, during the second wave of the women's movement, people became more interested in it. By 1972 it had passed Congress. But it didn't gain approval from enough states to become law. It still hasn't gained approval from the required number of states—and it still has not become law.

NEW ROLES

Still, women's roles were changing. The same year NOW
formed, the television show *That Girl* became the first show
to feature a strong single woman. And *Ms.*, cofounded by
feminist activist Gloria Steinem in 1972, became the first
monthly mainstream magazine about women's rights
issues.

Inspired by activists such as Steinem, many
women took to the streets to speak out for
reproductive rights and other issues.

GLORIA STEINEM became a leader in the women's rights movement when she published the 1969 essay "After Black Power, Women's Liberation." By the time she published the first issue of *Ms.*, she was probably the most famous US feminist. She went on to be a key activist in the women's rights movement. She wrote books, advocated for change, and continued to publish *Ms.* She was also a huge fan of Wonder Woman. The comic-book character was featured on the cover of the first issue of *Ms.*

CHAPTER 3

WE WANT EQUAL TREATMENT FOR ALL WOMEN

By the mid-1970s, the women's rights movement had achieved many successes. Many women felt empowered to take more control of their lives. But some voices in media and government said the movement had been bad for families. They said children suffered when their mothers worked outside the home.

Some referred to these opinions as a feminist backlash. Others called such ideas postfeminist. They said the goals of the women's rights movement had been met, and women could focus on developing their true selves.

In the 1970s, it was more common for women to hold jobs outside the home. But women still earned less than men and often faced sexism on the job.

A NEW ERA

Yet the women's rights cause continued to thrive. A new era of the movement began to stir. This third wave included feminists who felt the second wave hadn't been diverse enough. They felt it focused mostly on white, middle-class women. They wanted to fight for the rights of all women, including women of color, lesbian and transgender women, and low-income women. Women in these groups had needs that hadn't always been addressed by the second wave of feminism.

The women's rights movement slowly began to diversify as it expanded. These women march in Chicago for the Equal Rights Amendment.

Throughout the 1990s, women's rights activists worked toward increasing economic and career opportunities for women of all backgrounds. The first Take Our Daughters to Work Day took place in 1993. Its goal was to build girls' self-esteem and help them learn about careers.

Take Our Daughters to Work Day is now known as Take Our Daughters and Sons to Work Day. Yet a focus of this day remains introducing girls to various career paths.

RIOT GRRRL isn't one person. It's a punk-rock music movement inspired by third-wave feminism. Riot grrrl started in the 1990s in Washington State. It included female bands determined to express themselves as male bands do—and to express their dissatisfaction with discrimination. Riot grrrl bands included Bikini Kill, Bratmobile, and Heavens to Betsy. They sang about sexism, racism, and homophobia. Riot grrrls also published radical zines (homemade mini magazines) filled with feminist content. While black, Asian, and Latina riot grrrls existed, the face of the movement was white. The exclusion and racism felt by women of color eventually contributed to the movement's downfall.

By the twenty-first century, many feminists had turned their efforts toward health care and maintaining women's rights to abortion. In 2003 the Partial-Birth Abortion Ban Act become law. It prohibited certain second-trimester abortions, some of which were considered safe and medically necessary. In protest, marchers gathered in Washington, DC, for the March for Women's Lives in 2004.

A passionate crowd takes part in the March for Women's Lives on the Mall in Washington, DC.

WHITE HOUSE ASPIRATIONS

In 2008 Hillary Clinton ran for the Democratic Party nomination for president but didn't win. In 2016 she won the nomination and went on to become the first woman to run for US president on a major party ticket. She narrowly lost the election. While the country hasn't had a woman president yet, the results of the 2016 election suggest that the United States may be getting closer to electing a woman to its highest office.

Hillary Clinton speaks to supporters on the campaign trail in Cedar Rapids, Iowa, in 2016.

A Moment in the Movement

Guerrilla Girls started in the 1980s as a group of feminist activists in the art world. They remain active. Disguised in gorilla masks, they visit museums and other public spaces, protesting sexism and racism. They also hang protest art. Members wear masks to conceal their identities. They explain that they like to keep the focus on the issues and not on their own personalities.

Although the Guerrilla Girls started out as outsiders in the art world, they have come to be a part of it. Several large museums feature Guerrilla Girls art. And in 2016, three Guerrilla Girls appeared on the *Late Show with Stephen Colbert*—in gorilla masks, of course.

CHAPTER 4

WOMEN LOOKING FORWARD

Women's rights have made great progress since that 1848 meeting in Seneca Falls. But activists continue to advocate for rights. Many of them have joined forces with activists that support the rights of other marginalized groups, such as racial minorities and gay, bisexual, and transgender individuals.

Women's rights activists point to the fact that US women still make less money than men do as just one example of why the women's rights movement is so needed. As of 2015, women earned eighty-three cents for every dollar a man earned for the same work.

Tarana Burke supports the rights of women of color who've been sexually abused. She started a movement called Me Too to help abuse victims feel less alone.

FIGHTING FOR THE FUTURE

As of 2017, women made up only about 19 percent of the US House of Representatives and 21 percent of the US Senate. Women continue to work for justice on issues such as health care, paid family leave, and more.

The women's movement rose again in January 2017, when Donald Trump was inaugurated president of the United States. Many people believed the new president had anti-feminist views. Women and men around the world participated in the Women's March to protest the president

Barbara Lee of California serves as a congressperson. She's been a vocal supporter of women's issues ranging from equal pay to reproductive rights.

Crowds swarm New York City in this January 21, 2017, protest against Donald Trump and for women's rights.

and advocate for women's rights. The march dominated the news and called attention to the reality that women still have much to fight for. It also showed just how strong the women's movement is. The fight continues.

Timeline

1848: The first women's rights convention takes place in Seneca Falls, New York. This marks the birth of the first wave of the women's rights movement.

1869: Elizabeth Cady Stanton and Susan B. Anthony form the National Woman Suffrage Association (NWSA).

1870: The Fifteenth Amendment grants African American men—but not women—the right to vote.

1890: Stanton and Anthony form the National American Woman Suffrage Association (NAWSA).

1913: Alice Paul forms the Congressional Union for Woman Suffrage.

1920: The Nineteenth Amendment grants women the right to vote. The first wave of the women's rights movement ends.

1923: Alice Paul proposes the Equal Rights Amendment to end discrimination against women.

1950s: Civil rights activists, fighting for rights for African Americans, hold public protests and marches. Inspired by the civil rights movement, the second wave of the women's rights movement is under way.

1963: Betty Friedan publishes *The Feminine Mystique*. The Equal Pay Act passes, making it illegal to pay women less than men for the same work.

1964 The Civil Rights Act passes, which grants rights to African Americans and prohibits discrimination in the workplace based on gender.

1966: Betty Friedan cofounds the National Organization for Women (NOW).

1968: Feminists protest at the Miss America pageant.

1972: The first issue of *Ms.* hits newsstands.

1973: The Supreme Court of the United States rules in *Roe v. Wade* that states cannot restrict abortions in the first three months of pregnancy.

1974: The Equal Credit Opportunity Act passes, making it illegal for banks and credit card companies to discriminate against women.

1980s: After two decades of gaining increased rights for women, the second wave of the women's rights movement ends. The 1980s brings the rise of a feminist backlash and postfeminism.

1990s: The third wave of the women's rights movement gains speed, focusing on the needs of women of color, LGBTQ women, and low-income women.

2003: The Partial-Birth Abortion Ban Act becomes law.

2004: The March for Women's Lives draws several hundred thousand women's rights activists.

2016: Hillary Clinton wins the Democratic Party nomination for US president.

2017: Women's Marches in Washington, DC, and around the world draw millions of supporters.

Glossary

abolitionist: a person before the Civil War who advocated for ending slavery

activists: people who actively support or oppose one side of a controversial issue

civil rights movement: the struggle by African Americans from the mid 1950s to the late 1960s against discrimination and for rights equal to those of whites, such as the right to vote and the rights to equal education, housing, and employment

discrimination: unfairly treating a person or group of people differently from other people

economic: having to do with money and the production and consumption of goods and services

feminist: a person who advocates for women's rights and interests

protest: an event where people gather to express disapproval of something

suffrage: the right to vote

temperance: abstinence from the use of alcoholic beverages

Further Information

Alexander, Heather. *Who Is Hillary Clinton?* New York: Grosset & Dunlap, 2016.

America's Story: Activists and Reformers
http://www.americaslibrary.gov/aa/activists.php

Braun, Eric. *Taking Action for Civil and Political Rights.* Minneapolis: Lerner Publications, 2017.

Ducksters: Women's Suffrage
http://www.ducksters.com/history/civil_rights/womens_suffrage
.php

Fabiny, Sarah. *Who Is Gloria Steinem?* New York: Grosset & Dunlap, 2014.

Feinstein, Stephen. *The 1960s.* New York: Enslow, 2015.

Herda, D. J. *A Woman's Right to an Abortion: Roe v. Wade.* New York: Enslow, 2017.

Higgins, Nadia Abushanab. *Feminism: Reinventing the F-Word.* Minneapolis: Twenty-First Century Books, 2016.

Mead, Maggie. *Suffrage Sisters: The Fight for Liberty.* Egremont, MA: Red Chair, 2015.

Index

Photo Acknowledgments

The images in this book are used with the permission of: rob zs/Shutterstock.com (people background, protest background); Miloje/Shutterstock.com, p. 2 (grunge background); Milan M/Shutterstock.com, p. 3 (grunge border); Bettmann/Getty Images, pp. 4, 5, 6, 7, 19; North Wind Picture Archives/Alamy Stock Photo, p. 8; Adam Cuerden/Wikimedia Commons (public domain), p. 9; Universal Images Group Editorial/Getty Images, pp. 10-11; Stocktrek Images, Inc./Alamy Stock Photo, p. 12; Don Cravens/The LIFE Images Collection/Getty Images, p. 13; Bettmann/Getty Images, p. 14; © Gage Skidmore/flickr.com (public domain), p. 16; Joe Runci/The Boston Globe/Getty Images, p. 17; Barbara Freeman/Hulton Archive/Getty Images, p. 18; DragonImages/iStock/Getty Images, p. 20; Amitofo/Shutterstock.com, p. 21; Stephen J. Boitano/LightRocket/Getty Images, p. 22; Bilgin S. Sasmaz/Anadolu Agency/Getty Images, p. 23; PA Images/Alamy Stock Photo, p. 24; Chelsea Guglielmino/FilmMagic/Getty Images , p. 25; Paul Morigi/Getty Images, p. 26; Selcuk Acar/Anadolu Agency/Getty Images, p. 27.

Front cover: Jack Sutton/Shutterstock.com (modern protest); Library of Congress (Gloria Steinem); David Fenton/Archive Photos/Getty Images (women's liberation protest); Don Carl STEFFEN/Gamma-Rapho/Getty Images (student protest).